PRICE STERN SLOAN
Published by the Penguin Group
Penguin Group (USA) Inc., 375 Hudson Street,
New York, New York 10014, U.S.A.
Penguin Group (Canada), 90 Eglinton Avenue East, Suite 700,
Toronto, Ontario, Canada M4P 2Y3
(a division of Pearson Penguin Canada Inc.)
Penguin Books Ltd, 80 Strand, London WC2R 0RL, England
Penguin Ireland, 25 St Stephens Green, Dublin 2, Ireland
(a division of Penguin Books Ltd)
Penguin Group (Australia), 250 Camberwell Road,
Camberwell, Victoria 3124, Australia
(a division of Pearson Australia Group Pty Ltd)
Penguin Books India Pvt Ltd, 11 Community Centre,
Panchsheel Park, New Delhi - 110 017, India
Penguin Group (NZ), Cnr Airborne and Rosedale Roads,
Albany, Auckland 1310, New Zealand
(a division of Pearson New Zealand Ltd)
Penguin Books (South Africa) (Pty) Ltd, 24 Sturdee Avenue,
Rosebank, Johannesburg 2196, South Africa

Penguin Books Ltd, Registered Offices:
80 Strand, London WC2R 0RL, England

*Photo credits:* Cover: courtesy of Eddie Malluk/WireImage.com. Insert photos: first
page courtesy of Jeffery Mayer/Star File; second page courtesy of Jenny Maki/
Shooting Star and Stephen DeFalco/Shooting Star; third page courtesy of Glen
Harris/Photorazzi and Jemal Countess/WireImage.com; fourth page courtesy of
Eddie Malluk/WireImage.com

Library of Congress Control Number: 2006028055

ISBN 0-8431-2496-2          10 9 8 7 6 5 4 3 2 1

# zac attack

## An Unauthorized Biography

### by Grace Norwich

# zac attack

## An Unauthorized Biography

### by Grace Norwich

PSS!

PRICE STERN SLOAN

# contents

# introduction
## Up for the Challenge

To be a teenage superstar in today's world, where hit shows like *American Idol* and *The O.C.* mean that just about everyone is vying for a piece of the action, you need a few things going for you. Being adorable definitely helps. Having an awesome body doesn't hurt, either. But let's face it: There are almost three hundred million people in this celebrity-conscious nation of ours (never mind Canada and other countries, where a lot of stars are born). That means a ton of pretty faces and hot bods. Most schools—heck, most *grades*—have three or four prizewinning specimens.

Put Zac Efron in any high school in the world, and he would definitely be a candidate for the best-looking award. That mop of brown hair, with the sweeping bangs and sideburns that curl down cutely past the ears, might remind you of a young Ashton Kutcher. Zac's deep blue eyes, meanwhile, are somewhere between Brad Pitt's and the late, great James Dean's. As for Zac's body, he's nothing short of the full package—abs, bis, tris, you name it.

Still, there's more to Zac than good looks and a firm physique—all five foot, ten and a half inches of it. The French have an expression, *"je ne sais quoi,"* which basically means "something you can't quite put your finger on." In English we have another term: star quality. Whichever language you prefer, Zac's definitely got it going on. The guy practically oozes attitude.

But attitude, as you frequently see in Hollywood, can take a turn for the worse. How often do you hear about stars losing their cool, punching out some paparazzi, or partying a little too hard? Zac's attitude, on the other hand, is always positive. For one thing, he's probably the healthiest heartthrob on the planet. He starts out every day with a long, hard jog, and, as much as he likes the ladies, he's said he wouldn't even consider going on a date with one who doesn't treat her body like a temple, the way he does. As proof, Zac told *People* magazine in June

2006 that "smoking would be the thing that would make an impossible match for me."

To go along with his focus on fitness, Zac also keeps a totally healthy perspective on life. His parents had a lot to do with this, constantly encouraging Zac to take on new challenges, from singing to dancing to horseback riding to skydiving (which he hasn't tried yet, but really wants to!). The lesson Zac learned was that if you're afraid of failure, you'll never get anywhere in this world. "It's important to make sure you go out and try new things as often as you can," Zac explained to the *Plain Dealer* in 2006. "You've got to do what feels right for yourself, and don't let your friends decide for you. You have to realize your real friends will stick by you whatever decisions you make."

More than his leading actor looks, it's this "try anything" approach to life that explains Zac's success. While you may look at him now and think he's a born performer, Zac actually had to work really hard to get past his natural shyness. The story of his break into acting says it all. "I was actually forced by my dad into my first musical," he told *PBS Kids*. "My dad convinced me to go out and audition. I said yes, thinking it was a few months away and I'd somehow talk myself out of it by then. Little did I know it was the next day!" Can't you just imagine the look of terror on eleven-year-old Zac's face when his dad broke the bad news? Zac continues: "So I went into this audition kicking and screaming, and little did I know my dad had just showed me the coolest thing on earth. He opened so many doors for me."

Once those doors were opened, there was little stopping Zac. From bit parts in musicals to a recurring role in a hit television show to the lead role in the biggest movie in the history of the Disney Channel, Zac's star has enjoyed a steady and at times exhilarating ascent.

Through it all, the blue-eyed cutie has remained remarkably unfazed. It's often said of the best performers—whether actors, athletes, musicians, or politicians—that they make the job look easy. That's the case with Zac. When you watched *High School Musical* for the first time, did you ever think that Zac was once lousy at dancing and even basketball? Well, he was! During the height of the *HSM* hysteria, Zac appeared with his castmates on *Good Morning America*. The reporter asked about Zac's abilities on the basketball court. "Oh, my [skills] are nothing like they are in the movie," he confessed. "I'm not that great at all. I had one year of Little League basketball and I did so bad. I think I scored two points all season."

Pretty hard to believe, isn't it? Yet somehow, Zac makes audiences believe. It's the fact that Zac is true to himself and up for any challenge that gives him the power to play other people so convincingly. More than his terrific smile and fantastic hair, these are the gifts that make Zac Efron a superstar.

This willingness to take chances is the one thing Zac wants to pass on to the millions of fans who have come to love and adore him. As he told *TeenTelevision*: "My advice to teens is to try and do something that scares you every day because it's the only way you can test how far you can really go; whether it's going out and auditioning for the play or trying out for the basketball team, you have to explore your boundaries and see where you really want to go, and the only way you can do that is to break out of your shell." So *breaking free* isn't just the name of the hit song that helped make Zac famous. It's also a way of life!

# chapter 1
## The Early Years

Zachary David Alexander Efron was born on October 18, 1987, in San Luis Obispo, California. It should come as no surprise to hear that Zac was a pretty cute infant. "He was a beautiful 'Gerber' baby," Zac's dad, David Efron, told *J-14* magazine. "He cried if you left him alone, and he loved to be held."

The house Zac grew up in is actually in Arroyo Grande, a quiet, sun-soaked village on the Pacific coast about halfway between Los Angeles and San Francisco. It's a small, tight-knit community, with about seventeen thousand residents spread out over five-and-a-half square miles. The streets are pretty and lined with trees, while the houses are modest and well-maintained.

There's definitely an all-American vibe to Zac's hometown. Ambling through Arroyo Grande's historic downtown district, with its charming array of antique shops, family style restaurants, and mom-and-pop businesses, you practically feel like you're on the set of a Hollywood movie from the 1950s. It almost looks *too* perfect. Not that anyone complains! Even people who don't live in Arroyo Grande tend to love it, especially during the springtime, when the town hosts its annual Strawberry Festival. This fun-filled event draws thousands of visitors from all over the region for a few days of games, crafts, and of course the endless sampling of strawberry treats.

Arroyo Grande also has an excellent school system. In fact, Arroyo Grande High School really isn't that different from the one featured in *High School Musical*, the movie that made Zac a household name. It has about twenty-six hundred students. In addition to studying hard (the majority go on to college), a lot of the kids play for one of the school's many sports teams, which include baseball, soccer, swimming, and basketball. The school mascot is the eagle, and the sports uniforms are blue and gold. All in all, Arroyo Grande High has a lot of strong school spirit.

It's no wonder that Zac's parents decided to raise Zac and his younger brother, Dylan, in this idyllic, kid-friendly California community. "It's nice and warm, the perfect town for me to grow up in," Zac told *Tiger Beat* in 2006. Close your eyes and you can picture Zac, along with a pack of pals from the neighborhood, riding their skateboards or dirt bikes through Arroyo Grande's quiet streets, maybe stopping off for milk shakes at the ice cream parlor (though if Zac was as big a health nut then as he is now, he might have insisted on a snack from the local farmer's market!).

Growing up in such a carefree community definitely had a positive impact on Zac. He was about the most easygoing, well-adjusted kid you could ever hope to meet. "Outgoing, gregarious, fun, and very comfortable around adults" is how Zac's dad described him in the *J-14* magazine interview. Zac was also able to play the part of the fool every now and then. "He was in his fifth-grade class working with scissors and he accidentally cut off one of his eyebrows," his dad told *J-14* magazine. "He decided to make the other match. He really got teased about that by his classmates."

In addition to growing up in a great town, Zac had the benefit of a happy home life, and for that he has his parents to thank. It's sad to say, but there are a lot of stories in the tabloids and glossy magazines about parents of hot young celebrities behaving badly or treating their children more like employees than their own flesh and blood. Fortunately for Zac, his mom and dad have always been the loving, nurturing types. That goes for Zac as well as his kid brother, Dylan, who is four years younger—though you wouldn't always know it from the way they interact! "I treat [Dylan] like he's my age," Zac explained in *Popstar!* magazine. "As my dad says, I love to stoop to his level."

Despite the age gap, Dylan, who is the athlete of the family, has clearly been a strong influence on his actor brother. If nothing else, he's a constant sparring partner, always keeping Zac on his toes. Here's how Zac described a typical afternoon at home in *Popstar!* magazine: "[Dylan] will just come over and tap me and I'll sort of push him back and he'll shove me back and then I'll knock him back and then he'll push me until I fall over and then I'll get up and wrestle him to the ground—we're just brothers. We goof off and inevitably we fight! We have to fight, it's just in our blood, and I think we have the most fun when we're fighting." Boys will be boys!

Zac and Dylan also like to engage in the occasional practical joke, often at each other's expense. "[The other day] Dylan made me reach into a dark, scary hole to look for a golf ball he accidentally threw in," Zac told *Teen* magazine. "When I put my hand down there, he screamed, 'SNAAAAAKE,' at the top of his lungs. I almost passed out. He laughed." So much for the baby of the family being afraid of his older brother!

Even if the Efron household got a little wild at times, Zac's parents definitely knew the meaning of the word *discipline*. David Efron is an electrical engineer (he actually met Zac's mom at the power plant where they were both working at the time), so it's safe to assume that things like education and hard work are a big part of the

Efron family values. "I was always sort of a bookworm," Zac confided to *Twist* in a July 2006 interview. "I always tried to get the best grades, and I'm proud of that. In my family, if you got a B on your report card, it was, 'Shame on you.' It was a blessing, because that attitude stuck with me through high school." At one point, Zac actually boasted a 4.3 grade point average, even with all the advanced-placement courses his folks encouraged him to take!

Despite the challenges of being a showbiz student, Zac has had as much success in school as he's had onstage and in front of the camera. His dad, for one, isn't surprised. "When Zac really wants something, he can be ruthless in his pursuit," he told *J-14* magazine.

Zac has obviously had a lot of very positive influences in his life. There's one final factor that helped shape Zac as a person: his star sign. Zac's October 18 birthday makes him a Libra. Now, you may not be one for astrology, but a lot of the traditional traits that describe Libras sound like they were written specifically with Zac in mind. For one thing, Libras are often very good-looking people. Does that sound like someone familiar? Second, in addition to being beautiful themselves, Libras also appreciate beauty in others, which means they tend to be on the romantic side. It's no secret how fond Zac is of the opposite sex! Third, Libras are very social beings, and they tend to get along well with all sorts of people, not just the ones they have things in common with. That pretty much describes Zac in a nutshell. "In high school I really didn't have a clique," he told *Life Story* magazine. "I was more of a floater. I tried to hang out with everyone. I had friends in all the groups."

Clearly, the stars were aligned when Zac entered into this world. Throw in the great hometown that he was lucky enough to grow up in and the parents who raised him so well, and it's no wonder he's had such a charmed life. Still, nothing in life is just handed to you. It would still take that courageous first step into the spotlight before Zac could begin to realize his true superstar destiny.

# chapter 2
## Taking the Plunge

**D**ifferent kids reveal their talents in different ways. A future star athlete might show early signs of balance and coordination while someone destined to become a famous clothing designer will likely develop an early fashion sense. We already know that Zac Efron was a very outgoing child. But it was the way he always seemed to be humming a tune that made his folks think they might have a natural-born performer on their hands.

As Zac explained to The WB.com, "When I was younger, my dad noticed that whatever song came on the radio, I would sing along with it, and that I could carry a tune, which was really different than anyone in our family, because no one in our family had ever sung before."

In fact, although both of Zac's parents enjoy listening to music, no one in his family had been much of a performer. At one point, Zac thought his grandmother had been in the circus, but that turned out to be an exaggeration. "I actually found out that was sort of a fib on my part, because she wasn't in the circus," Zac said in *Life Story* magazine. "She was in some kind of traveling group, but not the circus. The picture I found was just of her on Halloween!" Oops! Sorry, Grandma!

Still, even if Zac's parents weren't trained entertainers, they knew enough to keep a close eye on their firstborn's talents, which were developing fast. "I used to sing the Tin Man song from *The Wizard of Oz* at, like, three," Zac said on *CompuServe TV*. "As I got older, I sang my favorite songs from the radio. My parents heard I had a good voice and they encouraged me. They both love music."

But as much as Zac enjoyed singing along to his favorite musicals, he wasn't exactly begging to get up in front of a live audience of strangers. Mom and Dad were persistent, however, realizing better than Zac did that what he really wanted was to perform. When the local theater group announced it would be staging a production of *Gypsy*, the hit 1950s musical by famed lyricist Stephen Sondheim, they strongly encouraged Zac to give it a shot.

"My parents thought that I should go in and try it," Zac explained to *CompuServe TV*. Zac, who was only eleven years old at the time, thought otherwise. "I had a horrid time," he said. "I was not excited about auditioning for it." But much to his surprise (and horror!), he landed the part of the newsboy. Though it was a small role, once Zac got a taste of the spotlight, you couldn't have dragged him away from it. "From day one, I got addicted to being onstage and getting the applause and laughter," Zac admitted to the *San Luis Obispo Tribune* in 2006.

*Gypsy* ran for ninety performances, each one more exhilarating than the last for Zac. From there, he went on to appear in probably forty or fifty musicals, including *Peter Pan*, *Auntie Mame*, *Little Shop of Horrors*, and *The Music Man*. Good times were had by Zac on all the productions, but *Peter Pan* was probably the most fun. "I loved playing John in *Peter Pan*," Zac told *Newsday* in July 2006. "That was a really fun part because I got to fly around on a 'fly' wire. I was hovering over people in the audience. I actually knocked off a guy's toupee once."

Looking back, you can see that it makes perfect sense Zac would get his start in showbiz through musicals, since they're what he grew up watching as a kid. When asked by *TeenTelevision* in 2006 what his single most favorite movie musical was, Zac replied, "Definitely *Grease*. I also love that show *Singing in the Rain*. It's so great, the energy and the dancing." Zac was especially moved by Donald O'Connor, who played the comical role of Cosmos Brown, best friend to Gene Kelly's lead character, Don Lockwood. "Brilliant," Zac said. "Everyone has to go watch that movie. It's so magic." Zac was so into that musical, he admitted to *PBS Kids* that he's watched the same scene from *Singing in the Rain* "probably fifty times in one night, laughing harder every time." Obviously, Zac's appreciation for musicals runs deep!

Even now, when aspiring actors ask Zac what they can do to break into show business, he always points them in the direction of the stage. "I would definitely say do theater," he told *Teen Dream*. "The way you catch the bug and fall in love with this business is to do theater. It's so nice to be in front of an audience and feel their energy. It really sparks your passion. There is no better way to learn skills—go out and try theater. Local theater is everywhere." (If you want to take Zac up on his advice, check out the Internet for community theaters in your area.)

As much as Zac credits theater with jump-starting his career, he always sensed that there was a bigger world beyond the local stage. From the age of eleven on, he started taking more intensive singing and dancing lessons. Once he reached middle school, he also started taking drama classes at school. That decision would prove to be the most fateful, since it was his eighth-grade drama teacher who persuaded Zac to pay a visit to Hollywood. "The teacher had an agent in Los Angeles and she recommended me to go down and meet them," Zac explained to *Teen Dream*.

So Zac made the three-hour drive to Los Angeles

to meet with a few big-time Hollywood agents. There's no telling how nervous he was that day, but he obviously played it cool since the meetings led to his first professional television part!

Things were really starting to happen for Zac, but the success wasn't going to his head, in part because his parents remained so involved in his life. Zac's mom, for instance, assumed the role of personal chauffeur. "Three times a week she drives me back and forth from San Luis Obispo to Los Angeles," Zac explained to *Popstar!* in 2006. His dad and brother, Dylan, meanwhile, were always waiting for him at home (though after a long day of auditions, there must have been times when Zac wished his prank-playing kid brother would get lost!).

More than ever, Zac would need the parental guidance and stable home life. That's because in the coming months, life was only going to get crazier.

# chapter 3
## On the Rise

**D**espite his obvious gorgeous good looks (a must in Hollywood) and his hardworking nature, it wasn't easy for Zac to break into show business in the beginning. All that driving back and forth from home to LA without any success took a toll on Zac's positive attitude. He remembers the feeling of his first audition—and his first rejection—for the 2003 film version of *Peter Pan*, directed by P. J. Hogan and starring Jeremy Sumpter as Peter Pan. "I'd never done a movie audition before, so I didn't come prepared at all," he told *Tiger Beat* in 2006. "I didn't get the part, but it was a reality check." What kind of reality check, though? Zac could have easily thrown in the towel and told himself he just wasn't good enough. But luckily, that wasn't his conclusion. "You have to do your best every time. But after each audition, you have to forget about it," he explained to *Tiger Beat*. "You always have to be looking forward and not looking back."

And that's exactly what Zac did: He kept on trying. It paid off. In 2002, Zac landed his first guest appearance on a TV show. He got a role on an episode of *Firefly*, a futuristic show about humanity after it abandons Earth, that ran for a season on Fox. Zac played Young Simon in the episode called "Safe," which aired on November 8.

That was just the beginning of a stream of roles on TV shows. In 2003, Zac landed a plum part in a comedy pilot, *The Big Wide World of Carl Laemke*. All the major television networks order pilots, or test episodes of a new show, to see if they like how an idea pitched in a boardroom actually looks on the small screen. Every year, the big studios and networks order way more pilots than will ever actually get on air. Unfortunately, that's what happened to this pilot, where Zac was set to play the title character's son, Pete Laemke. It never came close to making it on TV.

Despite that minor setback, the guest appearances kept on coming. The same year as his failed pilot, Zac was on the award-winning hospital series *ER*. The following year, he was on one episode of a CBS show, *The Guardian*, about a hotshot lawyer who ends up becoming an advocate for underprivileged children.

Zac kept trying like crazy to get a meaty part. In 2004, he went out for an audition for a part that could really test his acting abilities. Zac was actually one of the last actors to try out for *Miracle Run*, a Lifetime TV movie based on a true story of twin brothers with autism. He read for the part of one brother, Steven Morgan. He came prepared and nailed it. "I was so happy to get the role," he told *Life Story*. "I got the call and they asked me to do the movie. Within the next day or two, I flew out and began shooting in Louisiana and it was amazing."

*Amazing* is right. In the TV movie, which filmed in LA, New Orleans, and Atlanta, Zac acted opposite Emmy award–winning actress Mary-Louise Parker, who played Corrine Morgan, the mother of the autistic brothers. Autism is a developmental disability that affects normal brain function and presents itself in the areas of communication and sociability. In Corrine's case, one of her sons can't talk, while the other can only copy other people's conversations. After Corrine's boyfriend kicks her family out of the house, the boys are almost institutionalized. But the family sticks together. With encouragement from their mom to do "normal" things like play sports and do chores (and a lot of sacrifice on her part), the brothers eventually become students in a regular high school—an astonishing achievement that made for an uplifting story.

Zac—whose onscreen twin, Phillip, was played by actor Thomas "Bubba" Lewis—took inspiration for his role from a kid he knew growing up. "I actually pretty much had the character when I went into the audition," Zac told *Young Star News* in 2005. That's because Zac decided to mimic someone he had known over the years who wasn't autistic but had strange and different mannerisms. "I was always sort of imitating him in my mind. Basically I did an impression of him."

Like the conscientious student he is, Zac also read up on autism to prepare for this challenging role. He dove into

*Thinking in Pictures: My Life with Autism* by noted autistic author and speaker Temple Grandin. He didn't have much time to research since filming began quickly after he landed the part, but Zac told *Life Story*, "After a few chapters, I was more educated than the average person by far on autism." Knowledge is one thing, but acting rests a lot on emotion. Zac had that down as well. "I tried to just think about how each scene would go through their eyes. That's something every actor does. It's what you've got to do. How would the situation look from their perspective and their shoes?"

*Miracle Run* premiered August 9, 2004, and instantly received critical acclaim. Zac was nominated for a Young Artist Award for Best Performance from a Supporting Young Actor in a TV Movie. "Efron and Lewis are commendable in their performances for not resorting to stereotypes of the developmentally disabled," Ann Donahue wrote in *Variety* in 2004. "Each gets his moment to shine with a savant talent, giving the story the foundation it needs to wrap up with an optimistic finish." That's pretty high praise for a bunch of newbies!

The kudos didn't come just from the critics. Famed actor Aidan Quinn—who played *Miracle Run's* Doug Thomas, Corrine's eventual love interest and a father figure to the twins—praised Zac's fantastic performance. Quinn was especially interested in *Miracle Run* and had a lot of sensitivity to the issues at hand because he has an autistic daughter. "I was kind of amazed at the job they did," Aidan Quinn said of Bubba and Zac in the *San Bernardino County Sun* in 2004. "In a short period of time, they learned certain looks, ways of walking and holding their hands—things that are particular to autistic kids that, when you're the parent of an autistic child, you know inside out."

*Miracle* dealt with heavy topics, but of course it had its lighter side. "I wouldn't confine it to the autism aspect," Aidan told the *U-SGV Tribune*. "It's also a whimsical, funny film. We had a gas making it."

Zac had a blast as well, and he made a pal for life. "Bubba Lewis is a good friend of mine to this day," he told *Life Story*.

His career was definitely on a roll. But with all this

work, Zac's schoolwork became an issue. Although he's always been a great student (remember, he kept up a 4.3 grade-point average!), running to LA all the time to shoot his TV shows made it hard to keep up with public high school in San Luis Obispo. "It's difficult trying to go back and forth between work and school," he told *CompuServe TV*. "If I go down to LA to work, I miss a whole day of school. Then you're mailing all your schoolwork back and forth to your teachers, and it gets complicated." Zac would have to figure it out—since the parts didn't stop. By 2005, Zac had three years of professional acting under his belt. During this time in his career, he was still getting mostly guest roles like one on *CSI: Miami* for the episode titled "Sex and Taxes" (can you picture sweet, innocent Zac in a show with such a racy title?). But as it turns out, one of these guest appearances would turn out to be Zac's big breakout role.

# chapter 4
## Ups and Downs

T he entertainment industry is notoriously fickle. One season a show is the hottest thing on television, the next it's unexpectedly yanked off the air. Actors, too, have to suffer through these highs and lows, landing dream parts one day, only to be told a week later that their character's suddenly been "eliminated." For Zac Efron, *Summerland* was the show that would teach him this valuable lesson once and for all.

*Summerland* was the brainchild of Lori Loughlin, who some fans will remember from her role on *Full House*, the popular 1990s sitcom that made world-famous celebrities out of Mary-Kate and Ashley Olsen. Loughlin had created an honest, true-to-life drama set in a hip California beach community. She would play the part of Ava, a successful fashion designer in her thirties whose main focus is her career. That is, until her sister and brother-in-law are killed in a sudden car crash and she's left to raise their three young children.

Enter a trio of rising young stars. The biggest and brightest was Jesse McCartney, who played the part of sixteen-year-old Bradin Westerly on the show. McCartney's heartthrob status was already in place thanks to the years he'd spent singing in the boy band Dream Street and later as a solo musician. Next came Kay Panabaker, the beautiful, whip-smart actress who was chosen to fill the role of twelve-year-old Nikki Westerly. Talent obviously runs in Kay's family: Her sister is Danielle Panabaker, who's been in a bunch of television programs, including *The Bernie Mac Show*, and even appeared opposite Paul Newman and Ed Harris in the movie *Empire Falls*. Rounding out the *Summerland* cast was Nick Benson, who was awarded the part of eight-year-old Derrick Westerly. Nick appeared in the feature film *National Treasure*.

*Summerland* first aired in the summer of 2004 on the now-defunct WB channel (you see, even entire networks can get killed at any moment!). From its opening episode, the show established a kind of cult following. It may not have been on in every living room in America (in fact, far from it), but those viewers who did tune in were instantly hooked—no doubt instant-messaging their friends about this and that scene even before the episode ended.

The story of the three young Westerly kids uprooted from their quiet country home in Kansas and sent to live with their wacky aunt on the West Coast made for compelling television. "One of the things that made our show what it was is that we portrayed real," executive producer Remi Aubuchon told *Life Story* magazine. "The audience felt that we weren't trying to give them a lecture and we weren't trying to make everything cool." He and the other producers wanted to make sure the characters were living through typical things that happen to real people. "Then see how they solve their issues," Aubuchon said. "In a sort of unique, fun, 'lots of beach' way."

*Summerland* definitely confronted its share of issues, whether it was Bradin's adolescent angst or Nikki's conflicted feelings toward her aunt-turned-mother-figure, Ava. But the core characters could only carry the drama so far. Eventually, the show's writers had to introduce some supporting roles to keep up the momentum. Sitting around the writers' table one day early in the first season, one writer came up with the idea for another teenage character named Cameron Bale. They would make him fourteen years old so that he could fit right in the middle of Bradin and Nikki—able to interact with both characters. He'd be this sweet kid from the neighborhood but with depth, not to mention his own share of darkness. Oh, and just for fun, he would be really, really cute. The other writers loved the idea, and Cameron was written into the next episode.

But what actor would they get to play the part? He couldn't be a huge star, yet he had to have star potential. He had to have boyish good looks but also a soulful side. Sound like someone familiar? Zac definitely thought so. From the moment he heard about the part of Cameron Bale, he knew he had to have it. Remember what Zac's dad said about him being so ruthless when he really wants something? Well, you can just imagine how passionately Zac lobbied for an audition with the *Summerland* casting agents. Eventually, they granted him a tryout. Zac nailed it in every way.

"I went into the audition," he told *Life Story*. "Two weeks later they gave me a role, and this was after only one audition." Just like that, Zac was set to appear on one of the hottest shows of the summer. At first, his character was slated for only one or two episodes. But Zac was so good in the part of Cameron Bale and got along so well with his castmates that the writers decided to reconsider. Zac explained, "Before *Summerland*, everything I had done was just a guest-starring role and you don't really get to know the cast when you're there for just a day or two. Then when *Summerland* came along, I was just a guest star at the time, but slowly I became part of the cast."

After years of endless auditioning and countless near misses, Zac had finally gotten his first big break. In no time, he was elevated to a regular character on *Summerland*. Sparks began to fly almost immediately as Zac's character and Kay Panabaker's character discovered they might have more than just neighborly love. "The first scene I ever did on the show was a make-out scene with Kay," Zac told The WB.com. "Those are really tough, but everyone made me feel right at home. It was a blast because we got it out of the way. It made me feel like a part of the cast."

Once he was fully accepted on the show, Zac really started to understand how comfortable working as an actor can be. "Everything is completely different when you're around people like that," he said about the *Summerland* gang to *Life Story*. "They're like your family. And when you get to know everybody, it's more like hanging around with a bunch of friends. It's much more relaxed."

Though Zac got along famously with everyone in the cast, he was probably closest to Jesse McCartney. That's despite the fact that their characters were often at each other's throats! The two could often be found playing pool together or just hanging out. They no doubt talked a lot about Jesse's career as a singer, which Zac found really inspiring, though he admits he was also a little awed by the more established boy-bander. "I'm actually pleasantly surprised that no one's been holding me up to Jesse's standards, because there's no way I can fill those shoes," he told *Popstar!* magazine in 2006. "He's incredible. He's the boy right now. He's replacing boy bands by himself. I don't think I can be near his caliber anytime soon. I'm working at it, but Jesse's a step above everyone right now."

In addition to learning about the life of a singer from Jesse, Zac was always getting tremendous insight into his chosen profession. "I really got to see what acting is like," he reflected in *Life Story*. "It was a great break into the business. . . . I got to build a family with the people at *Summerland*. I would see them three days a week easily, and there's a strange feeling that comes with being on a TV show, and I got to feel what it was like and feel it out and test the waters."

Season one of *Summerland* ended on a high note for the entire cast, especially Zac. His character, Cameron, had been firmly elevated to "regular" status, and the writers were looking forward to developing it even more seriously.

Zac was wildly upbeat during the break from filming. He admitted to The WB.com that during that time, he was "all about the drama. This season, we find out that [my character] has some really deep and heavy issues. His father is an alcoholic and he's been abused. My plan is to run with that and bring in some drama, the kind that *Summerland* has seen before." Zac knew it would be pretty difficult to play such a tortured soul, considering his easygoing past and loving family. But he was up for the challenge. "Luckily, I've never had to deal with the kind of intense pain he's had to deal with," he told The WB.com. "That makes it exciting for me. I really get into trying to imagine what it's like to be in someone else's shoes."

Unfortunately, even as Zac was preparing for his expanded role, the network executives were setting into motion the show's cancellation. It was another case of "hot one season, gone the next." There are lots of theories about why *Summerland* didn't go far. But probably the most valid is that by opening the second season in the dead of winter (January 2005), it gave fans a major case of the chills. After all, it's a little hard to relate to a show about a bunch of people frolicking on the beach in swim trunks and bikinis when there's a blizzard blowing outside your window!

Whatever the reason, *Summerland* was officially yanked from the lineup in April 2005. Zac remembered the moment he got the bad news. "I got a call from a good friend, who is Lori Loughlin's publicist," he told *Popstar!* magazine. "Lori was on the line, too, and they said, 'Zac, are you sitting down?' and I said no, even though I was! I was actually playing video games. There was a big, awkward silence and then they said, '*Summerland* is canceled.' I had a feeling, but part of me didn't think it was gonna happen because Jesse McCartney's the coolest thing since sliced bread. So I had high hopes." But alas, the execs in charge felt differently.

*Summerland* had given Zac his single biggest showbiz experience to date. But in the course of a phone call, that was all ancient history. Not even a star as big as Jesse McCartney could keep the show from succumbing to the fickle forces of the entertainment industry. But as disappointed as Zac was, he had learned a very valuable lesson: When you fall off the horse in Hollywood, the only thing you can do is get right back on. Considering the storyline of Zac's next project, that lesson sure was an appropriate one.

# chapter 5
## Riding onto the Big Screen

E ven if it doesn't win him an Oscar, an actor's first feature film is always a formative experience. For one thing, making movies is a really different process than performing onstage or doing television. Think about it. While plays and TV programs can go on for years and years, a movie is usually shot in a few short months. That makes for a much more intense experience.

That intensity is multiplied many times when one of your costars weighs over a thousand pounds and runs almost forty miles an hour! That was the case for Zac Efron when he landed a starring role in the film *The Derby Stallion*.

The story centers around Zac's character, a fifteen-year-old kid named Patrick McCardle, who's from a small country town and has trouble fitting in with the rest of the world. His dad is a former pro athlete, but Patrick isn't good at sports, so there's plenty of tension there. And Patrick isn't very good at making friends with other kids in town. In fact, his only pal is a gentle old man with a lot of bad habits—drinking and gambling, mainly—named Mr. Jones.

One day Jones introduces Patrick to an injured racehorse he owns. Shortly after, Patrick befriends a couple of newcomers to town, a brother and sister named Jill and Chuck from the nearby city. Together, the unlikely foursome bands together to try to win the coveted State Cup Steeplechase. The movie has all the ingredients of a good story, including a couple of bad apples named Ronald and Donald who are intent on making life miserable for Patrick and his newfound friends.

Of course, Zac was thrilled to be tapped for the part. But looking back, he realized he didn't really know what he was getting into. "I've never done any horseback riding," he told *Life Story* magazine. "I assumed when I signed on for this movie that it was all going to be done by stuntmen. Then the first day when I came on set and talked to one of the producers, he said, 'Yes, you have three lessons and you're going to be jumpin'!' I guess that really turned on my adrenaline."

As we've already seen, Zac's entire life until then had been about taking on new challenges. So he had no trouble getting up on that horse. "I started focusing 24/7 on horseback riding," he told *Life Story*. "They had one of the greatest teachers come in and help me. Previously, horses were never something I thought I'd be interested in. The first time I got on the horse, I realized I was completely wrong. It's a different experience, and at the same time, it's fun! It's so thrilling and amazing to be on top of a horse."

After just a few lessons, Zac looked like he'd been riding horses his entire life—even though it came with a lot of bumps and bruises. "Oh, man, it was some of the worst pains I ever had in my entire life," Zac admitted to *Young Star News* in 2005. Still, some of Zac's costars had it even worse. Mike Nardelli, who played the part of a spoiled rich kid, said in the same article, "I've fallen off the horse twice, while Zac has not fallen off—yet."

Besides learning how to ride a horse, Zac and his castmates, many of whom also hailed from California, got to experience what life is like in rural Georgia. Much of the film was shot on location in and around Barnsley Gardens Resort, which is about an hour north of Atlanta. It's beautiful countryside, with lots of rolling hills and wooded areas.

The cast seemed to really enjoy the setting. "It's a nice change of pace from LA, with all its traffic and smog and all the people and everything," Mike Nardelli said in *Young Star News*. There were, however, the occasional moments of country-style excitement. As Colton James, who played another of the town's ne'er-do-wells, explains, "One time we actually had to do another take because there was a shotgun shooting in the background!"

Even with the occasional gunshot, the filming of *The Derby Stallion* was pretty calm. Zac was extremely grateful for the chance to learn what goes into the making of a movie. He also got to play a character with a bit of depth and darkness, which is great because he was denied the opportunity to do this on *Summerland*.

For the most part, though, the few months spent in Georgia represented a pretty quiet period in Zac's life. But knowing what was about to happen next, a little rest and relaxation in the country was exactly what he needed!

# chapter 6
## Disney Makes a Musical

**W**hen veteran producer Bill Borden came up with the idea to make a *West Side Story* kind of musical for today's teens—one that would appeal to both boys and girls—he had no clue he'd have a hit on his hands. "I wanted to make a film that didn't speak down to anyone," Borden told *Newsday* in 2006. The idea was nothing less than brilliant.

Still, nobody wanted it. He had shopped the old-fashioned musical idea around for a year without any luck. "I couldn't get anywhere," he told the *Los Angeles Times*. That was until he went to Disney, where they went crazy for the concept. They set him loose to make his movie.

To write a story that would captivate today's discerning youth, who are more used to Green Day than *Singing in the Rain*, Borden enlisted Peter Barsocchini, a former music-journalist-turned-screenwriter. Barsocchini's knowledge of music as well as his professional writing abilities were the perfect mix for the task at hand. It didn't hurt that the writer also had a twelve-year-old daughter, so he had a really good idea of what kids want from their entertainment. For his part, Barsocchini wanted to create a musical that would address peer pressure and how to resist it. "High school is such a polarized time," Barsocchini told the *Courier Mail* in 2006. "You've got the jocks and the brainiacs, the goths, the drama geeks; everyone has preconceptions about each other." He wanted to break down those labels through his story and the music.

The story that would become *High School Musical* definitely takes a nod from Shakespeare's famous play *Romeo and Juliet*, the seminal drama about young people in love despite huge odds stacked against them. Add to that a touch of *Grease*, John Travolta and Olivia Newton-John's seventies classic movie that brought together two high-school students from very different worlds, all to a rockin' sound track. Mix the two together and voilà, you've got a pretty cool movie.

In *High School Musical*, a cute, athletic guy named Troy Bolton meets and falls for a brainy (but of course adorable) girl, Gabriella Montez, while both are on vacation. During a New Year's Eve party, the duo find themselves center stage singing karaoke, much to their chagrin. Later in the story, Gabriella transfers to Troy's school, East High School, where she discovers he's a total jock—the captain of the basketball team, even! Gabriella is more the nerdy type (yeah, right), competing in scholastic decathlons. They connect again and get it into their heads to try out for the leads in the school musical. But everyone disapproves—Troy's teammates, Gabriella's bookish gang, and last but not least the performing siblings Sharpay and Ryan, who are used to snagging all the best parts for themselves. Talk about obstacles! Romeo and Juliet had it easy in comparison!

"The result in the story is that when the star of the basketball team admits he wants to sing onstage, it turns the school upside down," Barsocchini told the *Courier Mail*. "Don't judge a book by its cover. Don't typecast people."

Seriously, if that's not a super-positive message, what is?

Once the storyline was down, famed choreographer and director Kenny Ortega jumped on the *HSM* bandwagon. Ortega was the perfect choice to bring this project to life. He had choreographed the cult films *Dirty Dancing* and *Ferris Bueller's Day Off*. Ortega had also directed some episodes of *The Gilmore Girls*, which is a huge hit with teens. His pop culture credentials were definitely up to snuff, but Ortega, who was mentored by the late screen idol Gene Kelly, also had a classy background.

Ortega was really inspired by the message behind *HSM*. "I like the idea of young people coming to know their own voice, regardless of pressure from peers, teachers, parents, and society," he told the *Courier Mail*. "Too much bullying goes on and as a result kids back off from new ideas they have about themselves." He was also happy to introduce a new, younger generation to musicals. It hasn't exactly been a hot genre. "Young people don't get too many musicals," Ortega told *Newsday* in 2006. "That's what I thought was really fun about this, that we could go back and borrow from the classics, not reinventing the wheel, but do something for young people today."

*HSM* felt like a mission to all these guys—it was not just another movie. "I wanted to do something important," Ortega told *Life Story*. "I didn't want to do just another Disney Channel film."

Zac, who had grown up doing musical theater, was totally psyched when he heard about *HSM*. And he could completely relate to the character of Troy, a cool guy who follows his own heart. In fact, it was all the performing, singing, and dancing Zac did as extracurricular school activities that gave him that Troy-like perspective. "I was sort of in the same boat as Troy when I was hanging out at school," he told *TeenTelevision*. "Everyone thought it was so cool to be part of the basketball team, but to go out and be in plays at the local theater houses wasn't that cool, I guess. But it would be really fun to have your friends come and watch the shows because then they could see what the heck you're doing all this time when you're missing school and aren't able to hang out." A lot of times Zac had to stand up for himself and his interest in theater, despite what all the other kids were saying about it. He knew he had to follow his true passions and not the crowd.

But that's basically where the comparison between him and Troy ended. The rest was acting. "We're as similar as we are different," Zac told *Media Village*. "Troy is like the star at his high school. He's a basketball stud and hotshot. I was not like that when I was in school. But the way he is around people is like me." Zac claims that he was a nerd in high school, although that is so hard to believe. It's more likely that he's just being shy and self-deprecating. But the young actor insisted that compared to Troy, he was a loser. "He gets all the cool girls. He's like the dream character to play," Zac told *PBS Kids*. "Every guy would like being more like Troy when they were in high school. I wish I was more like him."

A lot of other young actors got wind of *HSM* and turned up for the auditions, which were especially grueling. The producers and director decided they wanted to cast a bunch of relatively unknown teens, not big-name stars.

"We're not famous kids," Efron said, describing the crowd to the *Chicago Sun-Times* in 2006. "This was just a bunch of newcomers who were trying something."

Zac's musical theater background gave him a leg up when it came to the audition. He was used to the sweat it takes to make something look right on the stage. "I had it easier than some guys at the *HSM* audition—some of them were passing out!" he told *Scholastic News*. "It was Broadway-style, seven-and-a-half hours of dancing, singing, and acting. And then we had to play basketball. I was probably weakest at that."

Zac, who chose "Let Me Love You," by Mario, as his audition song, was quickly paired up with actress Vanessa Anne Hudgens, who was trying out for the part of Gabriella. Vanessa had some Disney experience under her belt, having starred in the movie *Thunderbirds*. But this audition had some added anxiety for her. Poor Vanessa. In going for Gabriella, she was up against a lot of her friends who wanted the same part. The pressure was on, and there was basically no time to practice! "There were hundreds of us auditioning," Vanessa told the *Edmonton Sun*. "It was nerve-racking."

It didn't help that Vanessa didn't prepare any music to sing for the audition. "I spaced out and forgot I was trying out for a musical," Vanessa told *Entertainment Weekly* in 2006. Whoops. Well, she came out of it like a pro and ended up performing an a cappella version of Kelly Clarkson's "Low."

Zac was glad he was paired with Vanessa because they made a connection immediately while auditioning. "We were put together from the beginning," he told *TeenTelevision*. "To some degree, I think that helped us out because we really got to know each other."

Their chemistry mimicked the relationship between their characters, Troy and Gabriella. "There's people that you just click with right when you first meet them," Vanessa told *Popstar!* in 2006. "Gabriella and Troy just look into each other's eyes and feel comfortable. It's just like sweet puppy love!" What about between the real-life actors? More dish on that later.

He had the background, the smokin' body, and the great auditioning partner, but Zac still had no idea if he would get the part or not. The jitters clouded any perspective he might have had. "We were just nervous," Zac admitted to *TeenTelevision*. "I don't think any of us knew. The people that did know or did think they were great were the ones that immediately got let go because they were so overconfident. It was the nerves that actually saved you."

After a long and nail-biting process, the list of thousands of candidates was finally whittled down to just fifteen different actors auditioning for each role. The tension shot through the roof. They had to dance, sing, and act their hearts out for the Disney executives and movie director. "As they watched, they would tap people on the shoulder and send them home, saying they were no longer needed," Zac told the *San Luis Obispo Tribune*.

Zac never got that tap on the shoulder (neither did Vanessa, who beat out *American Idol*'s Diana DeGarmo to score the part of Gabriella), but he went home without knowing who did get the part. The producers couldn't decide between Zac and one other boy. It was the longest week and a half before he got the call that would change his life forever. Zac landed the part of Troy.

Now it was time to meet the rest of the cast.

# chapter 7
## The Friendly Set

**A**fter the crazy trial Zac went through to get the part of Troy in *High School Musical*, he knew Vanessa Anne Hudgens, his auditioning partner, pretty well. But what about the rest of the *HSM* folks? Zac would have to wait until Utah, where the movie was shot, to meet the other actors.

Well, almost. Believe it or not, Zac already had a friend on the cast. Ashley Tisdale—the perky blond star of Disney's sitcom *The Suite Life of Zack & Cody*—and Zac were pals way before either of them found out they made it on *HSM*. In the musical, Ashley got the part of Sharpay Evans, the high-school drama queen who hogs all the parts for herself and her brother. Sharpay couldn't be further from super-sweet Maddie, the character Ashley plays on *The Suite Life*. As soon as Ashley discovered she was set to play Sharpay, one of the first things she did was dial up Zac. Ashley was so excited, she screamed into the phone, "I booked it! We're going to Utah!" The two flew on the same plane, sitting next to each other in first class like bona fide celebrities (no champagne, of course).

In real life, Ashley's definitely not a bully. But she didn't mind acting like one. "It's cool to play a character that isn't like me at all," she told *Teen People*. In order to tap into the maximum meanness she needed to play Sharpay, she watched the ultimate movie for just that purpose. "I watched Rachel McAdams in *Mean Girls* for inspiration," she told *Teen People*. "She does mean things but always has a smile on her face."

Lucas Grabeel, a native of Springfield, Missouri, was tapped to play Sharpay's equally mean brother, Ryan. At first, Lucas wasn't that keen on *HSM*. "I thought the script was kind of generic," Lucas told *Entertainment Weekly* in 2006. "Once I met Kenny Ortega, I was like, 'This may actually be something cool!'" Good thing he didn't blow that chance. Lucas found some commonalities between him and Ryan. "I'm like Ryan because I have a strong background in theater and I did a lot of performing while growing up," he told *Newsday*.

The *HSM* producers made sure they'd filled their hottie quota when they enlisted Corbin Bleu to play Chad Danforth, Troy's best friend and fellow jock. Born in Brooklyn, New York, Corbin was totally psyched to play Chad, since he normally got cast as a nerd (certainly not because of his looks). The cutie who started out as a child model compared himself to his character. "Chad is a very passionate person about everything he does, which is something we have in common," he told *Newsday*. "Where we are not alike is that Chad is not open to new things. I love change."

That's good—since Corbin's life, and the lives of all the actors, was about to change a lot, especially the day in the summer of 2005 when they began the process of making *HSM*. Disney had given the producers a modest budget of five million dollars (that's a lot of money to most, but not in Hollywood terms). Although the story is set in Albuquerque, *HSM* was actually shot over twenty-three days in Salt Lake City, Utah. Director Kenny Ortega chose Salt Lake City because it was familiar territory. He had done the choreography for the opening and closing ceremonies of the Winter Olympics held there in 2002 (for which, by the way, he won an Emmy).

On the first sweltering day, the cast and crew gathered to embark on the most intense training of their lives. In two short weeks, they would all have to get up to snuff in singing, dancing, and acting (oh, and for some, sports as well). They had a top-notch team in place to guide them, but there wasn't a lot of time. "We didn't know what we were doing," Zac remembered thinking that first day (according to *Popstar!* in 2006). "We were thrown into a dance room and there were mirrors everywhere! We didn't know anything about each other and had to learn these dances."

The schedule was super-intense. For those two weeks, Zac and the rest of the cast would start practicing around 9 A.M. and spend the entire day doing exercises for singing and dancing. "It was really tough because I'm not a dancer," he told *Media Village*. Luckily for Zac and the rest of the gang, Disney hired dance star Charles "Chucky" Klapow to help with the choreography. By the time he was ten, Chucky (also the grandnephew of a Rockettes' choreographer) had mastered tap. He quickly added jazz and hip-hop to his repertoire. By age twelve, he was so good that Patti LaBelle, Celine Dion, and Salt-N-Pepa had hired him as a backup dancer. "He's awesome," Kenny Ortega said of Chucky to the *Daily News of Los Angeles*. "He is a master in the making. His creative instincts, coupled with his technical know-how, love for the work, and winning personality make him, in my opinion, the new choreographer to watch." Good thing, since Chucky had to direct the one hundred and thirty dancers in the finale.

The pressure on Zac to dance for a Disney film was made even greater when Kenny and Chucky enlisted the finest dancers in all of Utah to perform with him. They learned the routines at the same time. Needless to say, it took Zac a little bit longer than these trained professionals. More bluntly put, he told *Popstar!* in 2006, "It was pathetic."

As if dancing wasn't hard enough, as soon as he got done with that, it was straight to the basketball court. No loafing around or grabbing candy from the craft service table. Zac had to tackle yet another area—playing hoops—that he didn't exactly shine in (remember how he scored only two points during an entire season of basketball?).

The producer hired a professional basketball coach to put the boys through their paces. "We'd run basketball practice as any basketball team would," Zac told *TeenTelevision*. "We had to run suicides and all get in the layup lines and we'd run several drills."

Corbin has been dancing since he could walk, and he loved combining that with acting. But playing basketball? That was a different story. "Dribbling through the legs while dancing was so hard!" he told *Popstar!* magazine. "There were so many times when I would just start losing the ball." No kidding. While they were filming "Get'cha Head in the Game," everyone kept on getting hit with basketballs by mistake!

Zac didn't get done with all his rehearsing until 5 P.M. at the earliest. By then, he was dog-tired. "At the end of the day, I just remember being so beat and beyond tired," he told *TeenTelevision*. "I reached a new level of sleep every night. It was crazy." All that work really took a toll on the young actors' bodies. Vanessa's feet killed her because she had to do a lot of her dance scenes in really tall heels. Zac—who we know wasn't the greatest dancer when he started out—twisted his ankles, pulled muscles, and got shin splints. He had to chug Gatorade and pop a lot of aspirin to make it through the rehearsing. "I got all beaten up," he told the *Dallas Morning News* in 2006. "But it was all for a good cause."

Zac's costars ribbed him about his two left feet and lame hoops skills. Ashley said Zac did have the hardest time learning the dance routines, but she gave him props for sticking it out. "Zac wasn't the best dancer in the world or the best basketball player," she told *Newsday* in 2006. "Seeing him onscreen, he looks like the best basketball player and the best dancer." He did look *great* onscreen, but sometimes it took him a bunch of times to get it right. In one scene where Zac had to run into the gym and put his shirt on like he was just getting dressed, it took him three times to do it the way he was supposed to! You might wonder why, since this wasn't nearly as hard as a big dance scene. "My mike kept falling out of my shirt," he said with a laugh (according to the *Plain Dealer* in 2006).

For Zac, the best part of doing *HSM* was definitely the great friends he made along the way. With such a big cast and crew, there was always a lot of boisterous fun to be had. Who wouldn't have fun if you get to dance while working? The *HSM* shoot was basically like summer camp. That included a lot of practical jokes. "All of us did our share of pranks," Zac told *Tiger Beat* in 2006. Zac played one on his pal Corbin when he decorated his dressing room with a lot of caution tape. When Corbin walked in to change, he saw the place covered in CAUTION! He knew the culprit right away and started chasing Zac around the set.

The pranks, the hard work, and all the hanging out created a major bond among the *HSM* actors. "We were very close," Zac told *TeenTelevision*. "We're all very tight still to this day." To cool off during the long, hot days making a movie, they swam at the Grand America Hotel's pool. On their days off, they went sledding down the Alpine Slide in Park City or visited the planetarium. "We sat by the pool and we ate at every restaurant within five miles," Zac told *News for Kids*. They never left anybody out of the plan, so when they'd hit the local restaurants, there would always be sixteen people. And they all wanted to sit at the same table! "People would think we were absolutely crazy," Zac told *Popstar!* in 2006. The producers definitely facilitated the fun by hosting club nights where Zac, Ashley, Corbin, and the rest of the cast could get down.

Everyone involved in *HSM* knew they had something special on their hands. People had such a good time making the film, they figured some of the joy would have to come out on the screen. But of course they didn't *really* know how it would all turn out. Zac told *Life Story*, "The cast and crew were very excited the whole time we were making it, and that came through on camera."

Saying good-bye to all the excitement wasn't easy for anyone. When it was time to go home, everyone was super-sad, kind of like the last day of camp. "It was so hard not to be able to go to the hotel room next door and knock," Zac told his website zefron.com. "If I could go back and do it again, I'd do it in a heartbeat."

# chapter 8
## An Unparalleled Success

**W**hen *High School Musical* premiered on January 20, 2006, nobody anticipated what was about to happen. Zac and his crew blew everyone and everything out of the water. The *HSM* premiere on the Disney Channel, with 7.7 million viewers, broke a network record. But that was only the beginning of the stratospheric ride. Eventually, a whopping thirty-six million viewers saw the gang sing and dance their hearts out over twelve broadcastings (and out of those, eleven airings were the number-one household-rated cable show for the day).

Once *HSM* hit the airwaves, weird things started happening everywhere. The first time the cast tried to go to the movies as a group on a Friday night after the premiere, they were instantly mobbed by fans. "We won't do that again," Vanessa told the *Los Angeles Daily News*.

Vanessa and Zac innocently tried to get together for a trip to the mall. But they were hounded by a bunch of fans who spotted them and instantly broke into singing the *HSM* songs. The two young actors watched incredulously as this crowd of kids started doing the dance moves from the movie while they belted out the lyrics! While shopping solo, Zac walked into a Tower Records and the room immediately went silent. Yikes! Totally freaked out, he hightailed it back to his car.

Everyone involved in *HSM* had high hopes, but nobody expected anything like this. The young stars were in shock at how quickly their little musical swept the nation. It was in magazines, on TV, in the newspaper. People couldn't get enough of it . . . or them. Zac was definitely not prepared for his newly found fame. "I'm sure I won't fully realize until I look back in five years and think, 'Oh, that was crazy,' " he told *TeenTelevision*.

Vanessa definitely found one big perk to fame. "Free stuff!" she told the *Plain Dealer*. "Clothes. An iPod. I got a new TV from Disney, which was very generous." In fact, Disney gave each cast member of *HSM* a flat-screen. Come on, it's the least they could do.

Zac was just grateful that all this attention and fame could lead to more and better acting parts. "The most important thing is other opportunities to work, and working is really why we're doing all of this," he told the *Plain Dealer*. Nicely put, Zac (although he definitely liked the flat-screen as well).

No one, not even any of the bigwigs at Disney, can say for sure what made *HSM* the phenomenon it is. But its universal themes of being true-hearted, its cast of cute actors, and its great music all combined to create a rocket-fueled hit. "I knew we had something wonderful that everyone loved," Rich Ross, president of Disney Channel Worldwide, told the *Desert Morning News* in 2006. "I didn't realize when I said the word *everyone*, I meant everyone." Zac felt that the film was unique because parents and children could enjoy it together without feeling uncomfortable. The fantasy of musicals that drew him in as a kid now made millions happy. "There's something magical about watching big production numbers," Zac told the *Edmonton Sun*, adding that girls "love the romance, and boys love the whole basketball and sports angle of the show."

The movie wasn't the only smash. Disney released the *HSM* album on January 10, a week and a half before the movie's premiere, and in only a few days, it was on fire. David Lawrence wrote the score, but five separate composing teams were assembled to write the songs. In total, there were about a dozen songwriters working to make the sound track. It really shows, since *HSM* has an eclectic mix of songs in a bunch of genres from hip-hop to pop to ballads. With all that, they recorded the entire album in an astounding five days.

Zac was no stranger to singing. He'd been belting out show tunes since he was a tiny kid. "I've always been singing. Since day one. I started doing musical theater and you have to sing in musical theater and so that's where I got most of my training," he told *Teen* magazine. Zac also took lessons, but that was all long ago. He admitted, "Slowly when you hit puberty, your voice sort of disappears in a weird way."

Despite whatever qualms Zac might have about his voice, he became the first artist to debut with two charted songs in the same week on the February 4, 2006, Billboard Hot 100! "Get'cha Head in the Game" and his duet with Vanessa, "Breaking Free," were the songs that put him in that historic position. "Breaking Free" had its own trajectory: The song made the fastest climb in the Billboard chart's history—going from number 86 to number 4 in just two weeks.

And that meant sales. Crazy sales. The *HSM* sound track went double platinum, with U.S. sales hitting 2.7 million albums! Twice it topped the Billboard charts, and for three weeks, it took the top spot on iTunes. During one week, it had nine singles on the charts at the same time. No one was more surprised than Zac. "When you go on the Billboard chart, you're looking at Mariah Carey, Kelly Clarkson, and *High School Musical*. No way!" he told *7M Pictures*. "They have a typo here." Even the National Basketball Association got into the act, using "Get'cha Head in the Game" for TV promotions.

Could *HSM* get any bigger? Um, yeah. That May, when the DVD went on sale, four hundred thousand copies flew out of the stores on the very first day! After it sold 1.2 million in the first six days, *HSM* became the fastest-selling television movie of all time. The DVD had two versions: one had a sing-along edition with on-screen lyrics. There were also added treats like a dance lesson by director Kenny Ortega and behind-the-scenes bloopers.

The DVD release on May 23 was such a big event, it got its own Hollywood premiere, with a red carpet, glamorous celebrities, a party, and everything! Not many DVDs can claim that. *American Idol*'s Ace Young, *Dancing with the Stars*'s Lisa Rinna, and Zac's *Summerland* buddy Lori Loughlin were among the many big names who joined the *HSM* cast to kick off the DVD. Vanessa looked hot strutting the red carpet in her Betsey Johnson sundress and wild makeup. Zac played it cool (just like a guy!) in a green T-shirt and jeans. Hundreds of screaming fans lined the red carpet leading up to El Capitan Theater, where the hit movie was screened. Then the young stars headed over to the after-party at Hollywood & Highland—a thirty-thousand-square-foot, multi-level venue with restaurants and nightclubs—where they could joke around at the make-your-own video station featuring songs from the *HSM* sound track.

With DVDs and albums selling like hotcakes, *HSM* spawned a whole line of products. Disney released *HSM* "in a box," a set of materials that middle schools and high schools can use to produce their own versions of the musical. The president of the channel said they have already had forty thousand inquiries. There are *HSM* T-shirts, posters, and ringtones, and writers are hard at work on a novel!

The kids of *HSM* all embarked on a whirlwind of press tours, premieres, and promotions. Zac appeared on the *Jimmy Kimmel Show*, which he loved because he met one of his heroes, famed British actor Ian McKellen, who promised to give the young actor a tour of London whenever he came to town. Everyone in the cast was keeping busy. Ashley Tisdale quickly began working on an album, which she hopes to release in 2007. *Suite Life* fans don't have to worry: She's keeping her day job as the lovable babysitter Maddie Fitzpatrick. Meanwhile, Vanessa Anne Hudgens is also working on a record deal. But for now, Corbin Bleu is sticking to acting with his new movie called *Jump* (his dad is also in the flick!).

*HSM* hasn't lost any steam, either. It earned a whopping six Emmy nominations for outstanding children's program, directing for a movie, casting for a movie, outstanding choreography, outstanding music, and outstanding lyrics.

If Zac found his new fame daunting, soon there'll be no place in the world for him to hide. In the summer of 2006, Disney started to air *HSM* in about a hundred countries. In most cases, the movie was simply dubbed into the country's language, but in India the music is being rerecorded in Hindi with top professional singers. Zac would be adorable no matter what language he's singing in!

# chapter 9
## Onward and Up

There's no doubt about it: Zac Efron is one of the biggest stars of his generation. He's not just breaking free—he's breaking records! According to the *San Luis Obispo Tribune*, in the month of January 2006, Zac was the second-highest-rising Google entertainment search subject. In that same month, IMDbPro's STARmeter ranked Zac as high as number four (that's out of *all* movie stars, from Johnny Depp to Hilary Duff!).

As a result of his superstar status, Zac's face is being splashed all over teen magazines, and there are countless fan sites devoted to him. For the most part, Zac enjoys the attention. "I love the discussions online," Zac confessed to *7M Pictures*. "They can pick out things in a movie that you'd never dreamed people would find out." Still, Zac is aware of the downside of living under the media microscope.

"I don't go online that often. I try not to because it can either give you a big head or tear you down."

Not surprisingly, you have a lot less privacy when you're a major celebrity. Some actors handle this fact better than others. Zac, for one, seems to be keeping his sense of humor. "I was at a Cheetah Girls concert a few weeks ago and a little girl came up and asked for an autograph," he told *Teen* magazine. "I said yes and pretty soon the whole audience wanted one. So many people came up that security had to escort me out of the building. They sort of threw me outside in the back alley and said I couldn't come in until the concert started. Pretty soon my good friend Ashley Tisdale was thrown out there, too."

Shopping is also a little bit harder than it used to be. "One time I got trapped in a mall with a friend and we had to run to leave the place," Zac recalled in *Lifetime* magazine. "I have to say that it's also completely different for me to have people go online to look at my pictures. And people sign on to have chats about me! It's so alien. It's really weird, because I'm just a regular person. It all gets a little blown out of proportion. Not that I don't enjoy it, but it's just a weird feeling and kind of hard to describe."

But Zac seems willing to accept his responsibility as a role model. If that means reaching out to a crowd full of admiring fans, he'll do it. "Watching kids react is incredible," he said during a *PBS Kids* interview. "With kids you get a very pure sense of joy when they see you, and that's really fun. Because I remember when I was a kid—you used to see the people you look up to and when they sign that little piece of paper it made your day."

It's true—Zac used to be as obsessed over certain celebrities as his fans are over him. His dad remembers those days well. "We go to see the San Francisco Giants play one or two games per year," he told *J-14* magazine. "I have very fond memories of Zac waiting for hours for players to leave, hoping to get an autograph."

Although Zac is treated like a megastar by legions of fans, his lifestyle hasn't changed all that much. He's still pretty much the same old Zac. As he said to *PBS Kids*, "I don't have a fancy car. I don't live in a mansion. Everyone thinks that along with the movie you get rewarded monetarily. You don't."

After graduating from high school with the class of 2006, Zac did move into a new home in North Hollywood, but it's a modest apartment, not a zillion-dollar estate with a swimming pool out back and a bowling alley in the basement (though that would be pretty sweet!).

There is one other thing that Zac decided to pay for, and that's having the tiny gap between his two front teeth closed. "My teeth got fixed by braces," he admitted to *BIG Star* magazine. "What happened was the gap was actually very small, and when I went on camera, especially on TV, it would just distort it and make it look really big. So first, we shrank it and then we closed it all the way. I think my teeth look a lot better." Some fans might argue that he looked cuter with the gap, but whatever makes Zac happy!

What really makes Zac the happiest is working. That's what he's been doing most often since making it big. Though despite what you might think, parts aren't

# zac efron

**W**ho could resist that smile?

**Z**ac and a friend in one of his first red-carpet appearances

**Z**ac at a Disney Channel event wearing (what else?) his favorite necklace

**Z**ac with his idol
Paula Abdul and a
friend at a WB event

**Z**ac gettin'
down to his
hit song "We're
All in This
Together"

**L**aid-back Zac
chatting with fans

suddenly handed to you left and right once you're a star. "You know, everyone makes Hollywood out to be much more glamorous than it is," he told *Life Story* magazine. "You have no idea what the actors have to go through."

What they have to go through is endless auditions. There are probably ten times as many actors as there are available parts, so the competition is fierce, even for the A-list celebrities. "For every role that I have done on TV and movies, I've auditioned for thirty or forty," Zac told the *San Luis Obispo Tribune.* A lot of times, the casting agents will make it seem like he definitely got the part, only to turn around and give it to someone else. "It's ruthless. There are several thousand kids out there with brown hair and blue eyes that are my age trying to be in movies. Getting a job is like being in a casino." But as frustrated as Zac gets at times, he's not about to start compromising his integrity in any way just for the sake of a part. "I'm not going to be going out there having sex on-screen and stuff like that at this point in my career. I want to save a little of that young image that I've earned from the Disney Channel."

Plus, the fact of the matter is that Zac has been working steadily since the success of *High School Musical*. Some of the roles are large, some small. For instance, he played the main character in Hope Partlow's music video "Sick Inside" (Zac keeps his clothes on, of course, but it's still really steamy!).

Zac has also done a lot more work for television. He shot a pilot called *Heist*, about a gang of thieves who try to rob a bunch of jewelry stores in Beverly Hills during the week of the Academy Awards (when everyone in town is obviously a little distracted by other things!).

There's also the new show on Fox called *If You Lived Here, You'd Be Home by Now*, which is expected to be part of the fall 2006 lineup. It's a comedy about a group of people with different backgrounds who end up living in the same housing complex in Los Angeles. Zac plays the sixteen-year-old son of a single mother who is always struggling to make ends meet.

Probably the best television part Zac landed was a guest appearance on *The Suite Life of Zack & Cody*, the hit

Disney series starring the adorable Sprouse twins, Dylan and Cole. Zac was excited to work with the preteen celebs, but he was also psyched to be reunited with Ashley Tisdale, his costar from *High School Musical*. In the episode, called "Odd Couples," Zac plays a merit scholar named Trevor who is staying at the hotel where the show is set. Ashley's character and another girl both fall for the hunky Trevor, which kicks off a classic love triangle scenario.

Zac had a blast on the set, and he was really impressed by the Sprouses. "They're good kids," he told *Lifetime* magazine. "They're cool. They've got a lot of energy. They're amazing at what they do, and they're naturals. If I was their age, I would be so stressed out. I wouldn't know what was going on."

Filming the episode also gave Zac and Ashley a chance to talk about the most exciting news of the season: The executives at Disney had decided to make *High School Musical II*! No firm date for its release has been set, but there's been wide media speculation. It could be out in the winter of 2007—but it might be released earlier. Here's hoping!

There are a lot of rumors about the plot of *HSM II*, but it will almost definitely take place during East High's summer vacation. A lot of people think the action will occur at a country club that hosts an annual talent show. One thing is certain: The entire cast can't wait to get moving. Most of all Zac!

When *TeenTelevision* asked Zac if he'll try to play high-school students for as long as he can, he replied: "Yeah. I love it. I'm eighteen, but seriously, I'm operating on such a lower level. I'm young for my age. High school is a defining point in your history. Everyone remembers high school. At that age, there is so much drama and so many funny stories and great things happen. It shapes who you are. As long as we can portray this age group, I think I'm going to keep doing it."

As for what he's hoping for his character in the sequel, Zac told *TeenTelevision*, "I think there's not much more I can ask for. If Troy gets any cooler, he'll explode. I wish I was more like Troy. He can just keep on doing what he's doing." That may be true, but Zac did joke in the

*Edmonton Sun* that he wouldn't mind if it's revealed that "Troy is actually a secret agent or a superhero." That would really give him an advantage at the talent show!

Whatever happens, *HSM II* promises to be a sensation. But believe it or not, there's something just as big looming on the horizon for Zac. As much as he loves taking on teenage parts, Zac recently signed on to something that will definitely have him playing with the big boys.

# chapter 10
## Remaking a Masterpiece

Every generation has its hit movie musical. As crazy as audiences are today for *High School Musical*, in the eighties fans went almost as nuts for a little cult classic called *Hairspray*. The movie was written and directed by John Waters, who is known for his offbeat, often controversial style of filmmaking.

Set in the 1960s, the *Hairspray* story centers around a "pleasantly plump" teenager named Tracy Turnblad. She defies the odds and makes it as a regular dancer on the *Corny Collins Dance Show*, which airs in her hometown of Baltimore, Maryland. A power struggle ensues between Tracy and a rival dancer on the show called Amber von Tussle. Tracy not only wins the battle, she also wins the heart of hunky codancer Link Larkin. From there, the story line takes a serious turn as Tracy uses her newfound fame to tackle the issue of racial inequality.

Considering what a huge hit the original *Hairspray* was, Zac definitely would have been intrigued when he heard about the remake. He no doubt read through all the casting calls that went out in 2006, but the part of Link Larkin must have really caught his eye. Here's how it read: *LINK. Male, Caucasian, 16–23 to play 17. Broadway quality Singer and Dancer. The teen heartthrob of 1962 Baltimore. Sexy. Hunky, with an edge (like a young Johnny Depp or Elvis). If you think you are our LINK, we want to see your taped audition immediately. HURRY! All materials MUST be received by Friday, May 19!*

Zac didn't waste any time sending off his taped audition. Unfortunately, neither did a few hundred other actors. At first, director Adam Shankman wasn't very interested in Zac, whose clean-cut image he found "very Disney, very Mouseketeery," as he told *Newsweek* in 2006. But Zac persisted, and in the end he was able to convince Shankman that he could bring a "little bit more edge" to the dance. After a bunch of follow-up auditions, Shankman awarded Zac the part over two hundred other contenders!

Zac admitted to *Newsweek* that he's "pretty stoked" to be acting in *Hairspray*. That's sure playing it cool! After all, as successful as Zac has been in his career, this experience puts him in a whole new league. Just look at who some of his costars will be. Probably the biggest name is John Travolta, who, like Zac, had his breakout performance in a dance movie, the seventies sensation *Saturday Night Fever* (not to mention one of Zac's favorite musicals, *Grease*). Since then, Travolta has been in dozens of movies, earning millions and millions of dollars.

There's also Queen Latifah, the rapper-turned-movie-actress whose performance in the movie *Chicago* earned her an Oscar nomination. The list of topflight actors attached to the movie goes on and on, from Michelle Pfeiffer to Billy Crystal.

Some of the younger parts have gone to lesser-known stars, so Zac won't be totally intimidated by his castmates (not that he would be, of course!). The lead role of Tracy Turnblad, for instance, will be played by seventeen-year-old Nicole Blonsky, whose only credits include plays she's acted in at South Senior High School in Great Neck, New York. Compared to that, Zac looks like a seasoned professional!

Whether A-list or unknown, the cast will be in good hands. The movie is being produced by Neil Meron and Craig Zadan. The talented duo was responsible for the making of *Chicago*, which won a total of six Academy Awards in 2002. Besides talent, they have a lot of money to play around with. The budget for *Hairspray* is expected to exceed fifty million dollars. (That's ten times the budget for *High School Musical*.)

Filming of *Hairspray* is set to start in fall 2006, and the movie will hopefully hit theaters in the spring of 2007. Though at one point, it was going to be shot in Baltimore, the producers decided to move it to Toronto. A lot of movies are made in this Canadian city because of its gigantic soundstages and relatively low production costs. "When you do a big movie musical, you need huge soundstages because the sets are very big," producer Zadan explained to the *Associated Press* in 2006. "You also need a lot of ceiling space because you do a lot of sweeping crane shots, so you've got huge camera equipment."

Wow! This is all a far cry from the local community theater where Zac got his start acting almost eight years ago. Remember how he used to get excited about flying around the stage in a harness during performances of *Peter Pan*? Now he's got to get ready for sweeping crane shots! At this rate, it won't be long before Zac is making movies in a rocket ship high above the Earth's surface. But then, given how quickly his star has risen, somehow that doesn't seem all that impossible!

# chapter 11
## Just an Ordinary Superstar

Z ac might be a superstar with a worldwide fan club, but beneath all the glamour and glitz of the red carpet, he's just a regular guy. Well, a regular hot guy. He's naturally a cutie, but he adds to the attraction by being totally health conscious—he stays away from drinking and smoking, and he would never, ever touch drugs. Zac is also a workout freak: He exercises all the time. "After watching the entire *Rocky* series, I got hooked on fitness," he told *Teen* magazine. But Zac insists he's no jock, especially not while he was in school. He certainly was no team captain. "All I played was Hacky Sack!" he told *Popstar!* magazine.

That's not totally true. Zac, with his adventurous attitude, will try just about any sport. When he was in junior high school, he got into skiing, golfing, rock climbing, and snowboarding. In sixth grade, his first big splurge was an electric scooter, which he told *Teen* magazine "bankrupted me." All that zipping around was worth the financial strain. It didn't eclipse his skateboarding, though. He skateboarded everywhere when he was a kid, but once he started acting, it fell by the wayside.

One sport he picked up while acting is surfing. Catching waves became a passion after he spent long days on the beach shooting *Summerland*. The Christmas he was on the WB show he got a new board and wet suit as a gift. Zac must be amazingly gorgeous when he's all tousled from the sand and sea after a surfing session! He wasn't great at hanging ten right away. Once, he fell off his board and got crushed by a wave, which held him under the surf for ten seconds! "It was pretty scary," he told *Tiger Beat*. Not that it made him give up the sport. No way. "I'm hitting the waves all over the place," he told The WB.com. "We've had a couple of shark sightings, but so what. Here's the thing: If you get bit by a shark, you are the luckiest dude in the world because you are a legend forever."

If shark attacks aren't enough danger for our

favorite actor, skydiving is the next big thrill for Zac. He's dying to try that death-defying sport because he's always up for anything. Let's just hope he doesn't hurt himself on the way down!

Sports are only one way Zac shows he's still such a boy. Like most boys, he finds it really funny being gross. "I can blow spit bubbles with my tongue after I eat a Starburst," he told *J-14* magazine. "I've actually changed lives." Yuck!

Spit bubbles aside, Zac isn't above doing anything to get a laugh. One year, he went to camp and everyone was doing skits around a bonfire. It was a competition, and to get an award, the boys had to come up with something special. "My dorm decided to dress me up in women's clothing, and I had to get up onstage!" he told *Popstar!* magazine. They didn't put him in a dress, but he wore long gloves and other ladylike things. Then his campmates sang "My Little Lollipop" around him. Not exactly *High School Musical* caliber entertainment. "It was so embarrassing, but we won!"

On the more macho end of things, Zac loves to watch anything on Spike, a cable network geared toward guys. And he loves going to San Francisco Giants games with his dad whenever he can get away. But he's a big baby when it comes to horror movies. He can't take them because "lately they've been so scary!" he told *Tiger Beat*. Awww! Comedies are more his speed. Zac takes any opportunity he can to pop in his well-watched copy of *Goonies* and laugh his head off at the goofy kids' flick.

And he's not too old for baseballs, either. Zac says his autographed baseball collection is his most prized possession, and with all the money he's made from *HSM*, he must have a lot of great stuff. He told *Teen* magazine, "I've got almost every player from the Giants for the past ten years—except Barry Bonds. I'm working on that." That'd be the perfect birthday gift for the guy who has everything.

Right now, Zac has a new obsession—fixing up old cars. His hobby started when his grandfather gave him three cars! And not some old grampa-mobiles. These wheels are the slickest, even in California, where the competition is hot for cool cars. He's working on an orange-red '65 Mustang convertible and a late '90s Oldsmobile Alero. The Mustang is really rare because "in '64 they barely made any, so we have the first real year!" Zac explained to *Popstar!* magazine. But his hot rod is far from ready to hit the road. "I think my grandpa caught the engine on fire, but we're trying to get it started anyway!"

He's also tinkering with a silver DeLorean. "It's the car from *Back to the Future*," he told *J-14* magazine. "As soon as I can get a time-flux capacitor, I'm set." That's a lot of tough car talk, but in reality, his dad is the main mechanic. "I sort of just hand him the wrench; that's my position," he told *Popstar!* magazine. "I'm like the tool go-getter! He takes care of most of the work."

Between the cars and the extreme sports, you'd think Zac didn't have a softer side. But he does. First off, he is into clothes and cares about looking good. His favorite article of clothing is his Gucci aviators, which he called the "best present ever."

He's also attached to another present, a star

necklace he wears a lot. So who's the special lady who gave it to him? "It's actually from Paula Abdul's line," he told *TeenTelevision*. The *American Idol* judge put it on him, and he hasn't taken it off since. The star says, *Reach for the stars!* That's a pretty good gift from one star to another.

One of Zac's favorite ways to kick back is with a good book (he also has a major comic book collection). "In a few pages of a book, you can find ten times as much detail as a movie or a TV show," he told *Life Story*. Not that he has any problems with movies and television. "I love movies and TV. I think they're equally educational."

With his busy acting schedule and all his hobbies, it's amazing, but Zac has found the time to teach himself to play the guitar. He has a musical background. He took piano lessons for a few years. But like a lot of kids, he quit. Still, he took with him a few musical skills—including the ability to sight-read music. He's putting those lessons toward the guitar now. To speed along his learning, Gibson gave him a free guitar, which he's been playing nonstop. He told *Teen* magazine, "I'm starting to hopefully write songs." We hope so, too, Zac!

# chapter 12
## Life as Usual

S o what's an ordinary day like in the life of Zac Efron? There are some things that might shock you.

Well, first off, Zac's not exactly a morning person. In fact, early morning is kind of a blur for him. "I wake up somehow—I don't know if I'm on all fours, but somehow I make it to the shower and then I wake up in there!" he told *Popstar!* magazine. Once under the water, though, this sleepy cutie comes alive. Zac starts his day by belting out songs—but not onstage. These tunes are in the shower because he loves to sing while soaping up.

Zac says a perfect day begins with a nice long run. It all goes into his complete routine to combat the stress of being one of today's hottest young stars. "I eat right, exercise, and sleep a lot!" he told *PBS Kids*.

We know Zac is crazy for cereal, but he can't exist

on that alone. What's his idea of eating "right"? Well, Zac may be a lot of things—good friend, good actor, good-looking—but he's no cook. He eats sushi and anything else that he can order in a restaurant. But whenever he has to fend for himself for dinner, he resorts to the easiest recipe in the book: mac and cheese. "All the other stuff is too hard!" he told *Teen* magazine.

Zac's lack of culinary skill is a major obstacle now that he has his own apartment in LA. Since his career's taken off, Zac needed an apartment closer to auditions. So now he lives in that cool apartment in North Hollywood. He's tried to make it cozy: There's a loft bed with a couch and a recliner chair underneath where he likes to watch TV or dive into a book. That's when he can tear himself away from his two favorite gadgets—his iPod and mobile phone.

And if he's a bad cook, he's a worse maid. Zac definitely has a problem cleaning up. Really, Zac is a major slob. "There are dirty clothes everywhere," he told *J-14* magazine.

Sounds like the Hollywood apartment is 100

percent Zac. But that doesn't mean he thinks of it as home. No, home is still Arroyo Grande, at his parents' house. Moving out of his childhood home has been tough on Zac. "It's different. I'm not living in the San Luis Obispo area anymore," he told *J-14* magazine. "I've lived there my whole life. It's a transition, but it makes going home so much fun."

A lot of kids would kill to have their own apartment. But our sensitive Zac finds any reason he can to go home. And when he can't go back to Arroyo Grande, Zac calls his dad at night to share the ups and downs of his day. His parents, Starla and Dave, want him to branch out on his own. They're trying to help him become more independent so that he doesn't have to come home so much. It's pretty cute, though, that he gets so homesick!

Zac's not letting go so easily. "Being with my family these days is a treat," Zac told *J-14* magazine. "You have to remember as you grow up that friends will always stick by you, but your family even more so. Your family will always be inside your heart and by your side—no matter what."

Who can argue with that?

When he's back in Arroyo Grande, Zac loves playing with his pets, two Australian shepherds called Dreamer and Puppy, and a Siamese cat named Simon. "My dogs are crazy. They're always getting into some kind of trouble . . . but then again, they're my most loyal friends," he told zefron.com. He's so devoted to his pooches that when he's home, Zac wakes up at 6:30 A.M. to take the dogs out for a run even before the sun is up! Dreamer was his first pet, but in later years, she got really fat and had trouble running. "We put her on a diet," Zac told *Popstar!* magazine. Hey, just like a Hollywood star. "Now she's back to normal. She can actually run, so we're having fun. I'm trying to teach her to catch a Frisbee, but it doesn't seem to always work."

Despite his parents' wish for him to become independent, it seems like they miss him just as much as he does them. In Arroyo Grande, it's still like Zac Efron central. On the kitchen table, there are stacks and stacks of *HSM* movie posters, teen magazines, and newspaper clippings Zac's dad has collected. There are also scripts

Zac's considering and has brought home to read. According to *Teen* magazine, the young actor sums up this house as "where my heart is."

When Zac gets down from all the stress and strain of auditions, he doesn't just rely on his folks or the cozy confines of his childhood bedroom and backyard. He has another source to turn to: his best friends.

His main posse is made up of seven boys—Taylor, Shane, Connor, Chris, Bubba, Bryce, and Jorn—all guys he's known forever. "I've hung out with them all the way from diapers to this day," he told *Bop* magazine.

Zac's pals haven't been changed by his success. Well, at least his real friends, the core group he's hung out with ever since he can remember. Those who are jealous don't remain in his inner circle. In fact, he's the only one in his group who acts and sings. "I'm lucky enough to have friends that are so far removed from the industry that they do not care," he told *7M Pictures*. "I come home and it's a reality check."

They are a diverse group of guys. One of them is

going to be a professional basketball player. Another is headed to college to study computers. It's a real spectrum. "We're all very different, but opposites attract," he told *Bop*. "I never really had to look for friends because I always knew I had my buddies back home."

Just because they aren't in show business doesn't mean his friends don't have an opinion on his acting. Zac encourages them to express their thoughts on his projects. He's grateful for their comments because he knows they're real. "The best advice they give me is to critique my work," he told *Bop*. "It brings us all back down to earth."

When they get together, it's not earth-shattering stuff. No paparazzi or groupies. They just hang out and play cards like normal friends.

Zac doesn't see his pals from his hometown as often as he'd like, but when they hang out, it's like no time has passed or hit movies have been made. "I wish I had more spare time [to] hang out with [my] friends, goof off, be a kid," he told *PBS Kids*. "It can be a little tough to see my friends because I'm gone so much, but I'm enjoying it."

Text messaging helps a lot. Zac's practically physically attached to his phone. "One month I had around fifteen hundred text messages with friends," he told *Tiger Beat*. Wow! Luckily, he can afford the bill. And it's worth the sky-high cell phone statement. "It's just great to know that no matter what happens, I have my friends at home," he told *Bop*. "They are my comfort factor."

But what about girls? Is there anyone special who's part of Zac's comfort factor?

# chapter 13
## Love Life

**Z**ac's characters go by different names, but they all have a bit of the Casanova in them, from Cameron Bale to Troy Bolton to Link Larkin. But what about in real life? Is Zac as interested in the opposite sex as the hopeless romantics he plays on film and television? You bet he is!

From the sound of it, Zac has always had a way with the ladies, even back in elementary school. "I was in first grade, and this girl passed me a note in the middle of class that said, 'Do you like me?' and there was a box that said, 'Check yes or check no.' I checked yes and handed it back to her. It was really funny, romantic awesomeness."

Despite his early start, it would be many years before Zac experienced his first kiss—seven, to be exact, though beyond that, the details are a little sketchy. "I was in the eighth grade and it was with a girl named . . . shoot!"

Zac said in an interview with *Popstar!* magazine, forgetting the name of the lucky gal. "I can picture her face exactly! I can't believe I can't think of her name!" Zac never did remember the name, but he did recall that the big moment occurred during a game of truth or dare.

Game playing aside, Zac actually takes dating pretty seriously. For one thing, he's not the type to love 'em and leave 'em. "My first crush and I are still friends to this day," he told *Tiger Beat* magazine in 2006. "We text message and call each other all the time."

Zac has also put a lot of thought into the kind of girl he wants to be with. He's not the type to go out with anyone just for the sake of having another date. So what is his type? "I love it when girls have self-confidence," he admitted to *Tiger Beat* magazine. "If you can forget you're talking, and you look at your watch and see you've just spent two hours chatting, then that's when you know you've found someone that you could be with."

Apparently, it also doesn't hurt if the girl smells really nice! When *J-14* magazine asked Zac what makes for a really great kiss, he replied: "A good perfume. I like the smell of Pink Sugar." Got that, girls?

As for turnoffs, Zac is definitely into healthy gals, telling *People* magazine that he wouldn't even consider going out with a smoker. He also likes a girl who can focus on the conversation and not some song in her head. "If you're on a date, don't be constantly humming a song," he told *PBS Kids.* "I was with a person who was doing that and it was *so* annoying!"

Pet peeves aside, Zac's approach to dating is a lot like his approach to acting. Basically, his motto is that you can't be afraid or you'll never get anywhere. "Ask out your crushes!" Zac proclaimed in *Popstar!* magazine. "And when you do, you'll be so happy you did it! You gotta put yourself out there, because if you do, you'll have no regrets!"

Still, even Zac admits that he sometimes gets nervous before asking someone out. "It can be so hard," he said during an interview with *Bop* magazine. "The thing that's always going through my mind is, 'Does she like me at all?'" In those moments, Zac likes to play it cool. "I'll start up a conversation and not lead on at all that I like them. I get them talking and if they talk back, and we eventually find a connection, that's good, and if we don't, it's over."

One thing Zac doesn't do is hem and haw. "The worst thing to do is stew on the perfect way to approach a girl," he said during the same *Bop* magazine interview. "If you do that, then you think about it too much and you're bound to mess it up. If you just go out there and start giving hints and being yourself around the girl, hopefully she returns some of the vibe and you guys click. . . . Just go with your gut and be yourself."

Of course, Zac does admit that being a megastar makes it a little bit easier to meet tons of good-looking, talented people. "Yeah! That was one of the benefits of being in [*High School Musical*]," he told *Teen Television*. "Lots of pretty girls. I don't think there were necessarily any on-set romances. But we immediately all became fast friends."

Even if the cast members of *High School Musical* were just friends, rumors started to swirl around the set right away. Zac was almost always at the center of them! Some involved an alleged romance with his costar Vanessa Anne Hudgens, while others had him being more than just friends with Ashley Tisdale. But all three actors insist the reports were nothing more than rumors that had taken on a life of their own.

"Ashley is one of my best friends, and we're really cool," Zac told *J-14* magazine. "But I don't think we're going to be dating anytime soon. I think we're close in other ways. However, there's really no telling what the future holds." As for Vanessa, Zac admits to being very fond of her as well, but "not in a loving way. We hang out together. She loves shopping, so we go to the mall."

The rumors about Zac and Ashley didn't die down any when he made a guest appearance on *The Suite Life of Zack & Cody*. The fact that a lot of sparks flew between their characters in the episode only added to the gossip. The show's writers had a lot to do with that, sneaking a surprise kiss into the episode at the last minute. "[Zac] came in on the day we were going to rehearse and sees this scene that was just rewritten," Ashley told *Popstar!* magazine. "It was a total surprise for all of us. It was not in the episode at first!" Apparently, it took five takes before Zac figured out how to properly lock lips with Ashley. "Zac likes to do 'WB kissing' and that was not Disney-esque!" the actress explains, referring to Zac's steamy make-out scenes with Kay Panabaker on *Summerland*. "They said, 'Zac, you've got to calm down, okay?' " Not that Ashley was complaining. "It was good," she admits. "He's a good kisser!"

But even after the on-screen kiss, Zac and Ashley still denied any rumors of romance. "I think it's just funny," Zac told *Twist* magazine in 2006. "Me and Ashley are good friends. We just laugh every time we hear it! She's very cool and we hang out all the time, but we're definitely not dating."

So if not Ashley or Vanessa or any of the other beautiful actresses he comes in contact with, then who is Zac dating? For the moment, the answer is no one, but as he said to *News for Kids*, "I'm working on it." Though he's admitted numerous times that his dream lady is Jessica Alba, it's more likely that he hasn't yet met the perfect someone. He is even open to the possibility of love at first sight. "Sure, it's a complete reality," he told *Tiger Beat* magazine. "I think that would be a great way to fall in love! I mean, how can you go wrong with that!"

But just as Zac has never forced his acting career, only focusing on the roles that are best suited for him, he's not about to rush headlong into love. As he explained to *J-14* magazine, "I like to think I haven't been in love yet because I want that to be special." One thing is certain: Zac is going to make some lucky lady out there very happy someday—hopefully soon!

# chapter 14
## Looking Ahead

**Z**ac's future is wide open. Still a teen, he's got a rockin' career going that looks to have a long future ahead. But through all the hard work it took for him to achieve stardom, Zac never let his grades go by the wayside. Throughout high school, he successfully managed his acting career and schoolwork. When he couldn't go to public school because of his busy schedule, he had a tutor. Whatever the setting, he maintained a 4.3 grade-point average and graduated in the summer of 2006. "My priority had always been school first, acting second," he told *Scholastic News*. "I have a really high grade-point average, but if I hadn't taken the acting route, I think I might have been valedictorian."

He applied to two colleges, the University of

Southern California and the University of California, Los Angeles—both California state schools. USC has a great film program while UCLA is great for musical theater, so either would work for Zac. Surprise, surprise—he got into both schools. In the end, film won out and Zac chose USC. However, because his career is white-hot right now, he's delayed enrolling.

Although he's holding off on college for the near future, Zac doesn't have any plans to leave his home state. "I definitely want to stay in California," he told *Popstar!* magazine. "I went to New York and had an amazing time, but I couldn't live there. It's too fast-paced. California's much more laid-back. I'm just a California boy."

His dad is super-pleased with all his son's accomplishments. "I'm proud of his approach to acting, remaining grounded despite his success, excelling academically, and being accepted to UCLA [and USC]," Dave told *J-14* magazine. "It's [a] good feeling to be referred to as Zac's dad."

Dave Efron might be over the moon about his

son's career, but Zac is taking everything in stride. After *High School Musical*, everyone was chasing after Zac to get him to make an album. He had all those hits on Billboard and he plays piano and guitar. The idea was obvious. But Zac decided to concentrate on one thing at a time and hold off on the whole music idea. "I like to sing, but I'm not looking for a record label or anything," he told zefron.com.

If he did, he wouldn't want a team of songwriters and musicians to whip up a phony album for him. "I would really put my heart and soul into an album," he told *Teen* magazine. "I would sit down with a guitar and write eleven or twelve good songs for an album, and that is gonna take a long time." Don't hold your breath for Zac's album. He's focusing on acting for the time being. He wants to build a true and solid foundation for his career. "The most important thing is to establish myself as an actor," he told *TeenTelevision*.

In terms of future film projects, Zac dreams about working with the best actors in the business. Two actresses on the top of his list are Reese Witherspoon and Catherine Zeta-Jones. Whether that's for their acting talents or their beauty, he'll never tell.

But Zac does have another secret passion: directing. "As much as it's a performing art, I'm not really a performer," he told *TeenTelevision*. "I want to be behind the camera." Zac, not a performer? Wow, he fooled half the universe with that one. Zac fans, don't worry that he's throwing in the towel on his acting career anytime soon. "I would like to make my mark in front of the camera first before I endeavor to get behind it." Phew!

In fact, when asked by *PBS Kids* where he saw himself in ten years, Zac said, "I'd like to see myself still doing this. *High School Musical Number 48*." Amen to that!

# chapter 15
## Fun, Fast Facts

A re you Zac's biggest fan? Is your room papered with pictures of the *High School Musical* cutie? Can you sing every lyric from his *HSM* songs? Well, test your knowledge of all things Zac and see how many of the following facts you already know.

1   Name: Zachary David Alexander Efron
2.  Birth date: Sunday, October 18, 1987
3.  Birthplace: San Luis Obispo, California
4.  Current home: Hollywood
5.  Zodiac sign: Libra
6.  Parents: David and Starla
7.  Siblings: Dylan
8.  Pets: Two Australian shepherds, Dreamer and Puppy, and a Siamese cat, Simon
9.  Favorite cartoon: *Rocco's Modern Life*

10 Most prized possession: His autographed baseball collection

11. Favorite book: *Robinson Crusoe,* by Daniel Defoe

12. Favorite movie: *Goonies* and *Dumb and Dumber*

13. Dream role: Spider-Man

14. Favorite TV show: *Most Extreme Elimination* and *That '70s Show*

15. Favorite fast-food snack: Honey mustard chicken sandwich with bacon from Quiznos. "You know heaven?" Zac said. "It's kinda like that!"

16. Celebrity whose autograph Zac most wants: Los Angeles Lakers guard Kobe Bryant

17. Dream car: Toyota Supra from *The Fast and the Furious*

18. Zac has prescription contact lenses but never wears them.

# chapter 16
## Zac's Discography

**E**ven before Zac was talking in complete sentences, he was humming along to his favorite tunes. As he got older, listening to music definitely evolved into one of his favorite hobbies. Though he's talked about maybe someday pursuing a career in music (especially after hanging out with rocker Jesse McCartney on the set of *Summerland*), for the moment, he's just a fan. But he's a *huge* fan. In fact, whether he's filming a movie or just kicking back at home, Zac is never far from his iPod. Though he's probably downloaded thousands of songs, here's a sampling of the musicians and sound tracks that Zac considers his current favorites.

## Jack Johnson

This Hawaii-born singer and songwriter used to be a professional surfer, so it's no wonder Zac's a fan! Johnson was in a pretty bad surfing accident a while back, and it was during his recovery that he started penning songs and playing the guitar. His music is totally laid-back and mellow, the kind of stuff that's perfect to listen to on the beach as the sun's going down—which Zac no doubt does all the time! Johnson's 2003 album, *On and On*, debuted at number three on the Billboard 200 on the strength of its hit single "The Horizon Has Been Defeated." Check it out!

## Ben Harper

Harper's music is also super-chill. The California native actually took Jack Johnson under his wing at one time, so it's no wonder they have similar sounds and that Zac digs them both equally. As his latest album, *Both Sides of the Gun*, proves, Harper is a little more versatile than Johnson. Sometimes he's folksy, sometimes he's bluesy, and sometimes he rocks it out. But as far as Zac is concerned, he's always totally awesome!

## John Mayer

This twenty-eight-year-old singer-songwriter is probably best known for his song "Your Body Is a Wonderland," from the album *Room for Squares*. The catchy single won him the Grammy Award for Best Male Pop Vocal Performance in 2003. He's another artist known for soulful lyrics and soft, melodious guitar playing. Mayer's tunes are usually really romantic—perfect "date music," as Zac has no doubt discovered!

## The Shins

This band consists of four guys from Albuquerque, New Mexico, though they now call Portland, Oregon, home. Their sound is usually described as "indie rock." It's inspired by many different music genres, including pop, alternative, folk, and even country. Two tracks from The Shins' album *Oh, Inverted World* are on the sound track to the movie *Garden State* (which is another one of Zac's favorites). The track "Know Your Onion!" was used on an episode of *Gilmore Girls*, and the band even appeared on the show!

## Avenue Q Sound Track

By far, the tunes that are getting the most play from Zac are those featured on the sound track to the hit Broadway musical *Avenue Q*. "Like the top twenty-five most-played songs on my iPod are from that play!" he told *Popstar!* magazine. The musical tells the story of a recent Princeton grad who comes to New York City to make it big (Avenue Q is the name of the neighborhood where he ends up living). It features one hit song-and-dance routine after another—and Zac loves them all!

## The Postal Service

While *Avenue Q* keeps Zac happy, when his spirits are low, he turns to another album. "When I'm down, I listen to The Postal Service," he admitted to *Tiger Beat* magazine. The band's name, in case you're curious, refers to the way its members would trade tapes and music by mail. The music definitely couldn't be described as happy, with its gut-wrenching lyrics and brooding melodies. But even Zac has his down moments, and it's the perfect music to go along with them.

## Coldplay

Zac is really into international music, including this alternative rock band from London, England. They're pretty well-known in the United States, in part because their lead singer, Chris Martin, is married to famous actress Gwyneth Paltrow. Coldplay songs contain the introspective lyrics that Zac obviously looks for in a band. It's no wonder Coldplay features prominently on his personal playlist.

# Matt Costa

This is one of Zac's more recent discoveries. Matt was initially a skateboarder, but an awful accident ended his career. Just as Jack Johnson did after he hurt himself surfing, Matt started making music while he was recovering from his injury. At first, he only shared the results with close friends in his California hometown. But the songs were so good that his reputation quickly spread. Always in the know, Zac was quick to hear about the up-and-coming star, and he's been listening ever since.

# *Hairspray* Sound Track

Listening to the original sound track from this movie musical is part pleasure, part work, since Zac is all set to play the part of Link Larkin in the upcoming remake. Zac always researches his roles thoroughly, so he definitely has every lyric from every tune memorized by now. It's going to be awesome to hear his own renditions of the songs!

# chapter 17
## Online Sightings

Zac is full of energy and on the go in every way. In only a few years, his life has changed radically from that of a young kid doing regional musical theater to that of an international celebrity. His whirlwind style doesn't show any signs of petering out. So if you want to catch up on the latest news about Zac, check out the sites listed below. You should always get a parent's permission before signing online, and keep in mind that websites are always coming and going!

Official Zac Efron website:

**www.zefron.com**

Zac Efron picture gallery:

**zac-efron-picture.blogspot.com**

Internet Movie Database:
**www.imdb.com/name/nm1374980**

The Zac Efron forum on the official Disney Channel:
**disneychannelforum.jconserv.net**

*High School Musical* fan site:
**www.freewebs.com/**
**highschoolmusicalfanforlife8907**

*High School Musical* site:
**www.disneychannel.com**